JANICE VANCLEAVE'S
PLANTS

JANICE VANCLEAVE'S A+ PROJECTS

A+ Projects in Biology   A+ Projects in Chemistry

JANICE VANCLEAVE'S
SPECTACULAR SCIENCE PROJECTS

Animals   Microscopes and Magnifying Lenses
Earthquakes   Molecules
Electricity   Rocks and Minerals
Gravity   Volcanoes
Machines   Weather
Magnets

JANICE VANCLEAVE'S
SCIENCE FOR EVERY KID SERIES

Astronomy for Every Kid
Biology for Every Kid
Chemistry for Every Kid
Dinosaurs for Every Kid
Earth Science for Every Kid
Ecology for Every Kid
Geography for Every Kid
Geometry for Every Kid
The Human Body for Every Kid
Math for Every Kid
Physics for Every Kid

Spectacular Science Projects

Janice VanCleave's
Plants

MIND-BOGGLING EXPERIMENTS YOU CAN TURN INTO SCIENCE FAIR PROJECTS

John Wiley & Sons, Inc.
New York • Chichester • Brisbane • Toronto • Singapore • Weinheim

Copyright © 1997 by Janice VanCleave
Published by John Wiley & Sons, Inc.

Library of Congress Cataloging-in-Publication Data
VanCleave, Janice Pratt.
   Janice VanCleave's plants : mind-boggling experiments you can turn
into science fair projects.
      p.   cm. — (Spectacular science projects)
   Includes index.
   Summary: Presents facts about plants and includes experiments,
projects, and activities related to each topic.
   ISBN 0-471-14687-0 (pbk. : alk. paper)
   1. Botany—Experiments—Juvenile literature. 2. Plants—
Experiments—Juvenile literature. 3. Botany projects—Juvenile
literature. [1. Botany—Experiments. 2. Plants—Experiments.
3. Experiments. 4. Science projects.]   I. Title. II. Series:
VanCleave, Janice Pratt. Janice VanCleave's spectacular science
projects.
QK52.6.V35   1996
581—dc20   96–2744

Printed in the United States of America
10 9 8 7 6 5 4 3 2 1

CONTENTS

DEDICATION

This book is dedicated to Laura Fields Roberts, a lady who receives an A+ rating as a field tester. To make her timed observations, this dedicated worker took cups of growing beans and an alarm clock with her when she attended an all-day meeting on technology activities development. The alarm was slightly distracting at the time, but the other attendees good-naturedly stopped while Laura measured the beans. Some of them still curiously inquire about her current experiments.

Laura was assisted in field-testing this book by Jim Roberts, her special helpmate. He not only did plant sitting, but was a technical consultant as well. Nettie Fields, her mom, and Mary Sue McCune provided encouragement and necessary plants.

Thanks, Laura, for all your wonderful help.

ACKNOWLEDGMENTS

I would like to thank my husband, Wade, for his patience during the writing of this book. The collection of materials around our house always gives clues to the subject matter of the book I am writing. While writing this plant book, we lived in what appeared to be an unusual greenhouse, with plastic cups of growing seeds on most flat surfaces, and plastic bags of growing seeds taped to windows. I'll not elaborate on the things in the refrigerator. Wade is a very understanding husband. I hope he stays that way, because my next book will be about insects and spiders.

Introduction

Science is a search for answers. Science projects are good ways to learn more about science as you search for the answers to specific problems. This book will give you guidance and provide ideas, but you must do your part in the search by planning experiments, finding and recording information related to the problem, and organizing the data collected to find the answer to the problem.

Sharing your findings by presenting your project at science fairs will be a rewarding experience if you have properly prepared for the exhibit. Trying to assemble a project overnight results in frustration, and you cheat yourself out of the fun of being a science detective. Solving a scientific mystery, like solving a detective mystery, requires planning and the careful collecting of facts. The following sections provide suggestions for how to get started on this scientific quest. Start the project with curiosity and a desire to learn something new.

SELECT A TOPIC

Each of the 20 chapters in this book focuses on a specific topic and suggests many possible problems to solve. Each chapter begins with one "cookbook" experiment—follow the recipe and the result is guaranteed. Approximate metric equivalents have been given after all English measurements. Try several or all of these easy

experiments before choosing the topic you like best and want to know more about. Regardless of the problem you choose to solve, what you discover will make you more knowledgeable about plants.

KEEP A JOURNAL

Purchase a bound notebook in which to write everything related to the project. This is your journal. It will contain your original ideas as well as ideas you get from books or from people like teachers and scientists. It will include descriptions of your experiments as well as diagrams, photographs, and written observations of all your results. Every entry should be as neat as possible, and dated. Information from this journal can be used to write a report of your project, and you will want to display the journal with your completed project. A neat, orderly journal provides a complete and accurate record of your project from start to finish. It is also proof of the time you spent sleuthing out the answers to the scientific mystery you undertook to solve.

LET'S EXPLORE

This section of each chapter follows the original experiment that introduces the chapter and provides additional questions about the problem presented in the experiment. By making small changes to some part of the original experiment, new results are achieved. Think about why these new results might have happened.

SHOW TIME!

This section goes a step further than "Let's Explore" by offering more ideas for problems to solve and questions to answer related to the general topic of the chapter. You can use the format of the original experiment to design your own experiments to solve the questions and explore the suggestions in "Let's Explore" and "Show Time!" Your own experiment should follow the original experiment's format and include a single question about one idea, a list of necessary materials, a detailed step-by-step procedure, written results with diagrams, graphs, and charts if they seem helpful, and a conclusion answering and explaining the question. Include any information you found through research to clarify your answer. When you design your own experiments, make sure to get an adult's approval if supplies or procedures other than those given in this book are used.

If you want to make a science fair project, study the information listed here and after each experiment in the book to develop your ideas into a real science fair exhibit. Use the suggestions that best apply to the project topic that you have chosen. Keep in mind that while your display represents all the work that you have done, it must tell the story of the project in such a way that it attracts and holds the interest of the viewer. So keep it simple. Do not try to cram all of your information into one place. To have more space on the display and still exhibit all your work, keep some of the charts, graphs, pictures, and other materials in your journal instead of on the display board itself.

The actual size and shape of displays can be different from those stated in this book, depending on your local science fair officials, so you will have to check the rules for your science fair. Most exhibits can be 48 inches (122 cm) wide, 30 inches (76 cm) deep, and 108 inches (274 cm) high. These are maximum measurements and your display may be smaller than this. A three-sided backboard, as shown here, is usually the best way to display your work. Wooden panels can be hinged together, but you can also use sturdy cardboard pieces taped together to form a very inexpensive but presentable exhibit.

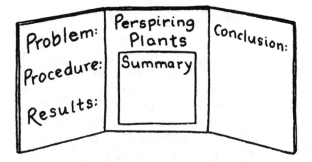

A good title of six words or less with a maximum of 50 characters should be placed at the top of the center panel. The title should capture the theme of the project but should not be the same as the problem statements. For example, if the problem under question is *How do plants get rid of excess water?*, a good title of the project may be "Perspiring Plants." The title and other headings should be neat and large enough to be readable at a distance of about 3 feet (1 m). You can glue letters to the backboard (you can use precut letters that you buy or letters that you cut out of construction paper), or you can stencil the letters for all the titles. Directly under the title, add a short summary paragraph of about 100 words to explain the scientific principles involved. A person who has no knowledge of the topic should be able to easily understand the basic idea of the project just from reading the summary.

There are no set rules about the position of the information on the display. However, it all needs to be well organized. The title and summary paragraph should be centered at the top as the main point and the remaining material placed neatly from left to right under specific headings. Choices of headings will depend on how you wish to display the information. Separate headings for Problem, Procedure, Results, and Conclusion may be used.

The judges give points for how clearly you are able to discuss the project and explain its purpose, procedure, results, and conclusion. The display should be organized so that it explains everything, but your ability to discuss your project and answer the questions of the judges convinces them that you did the work and understand what you have done. Practice a speech in front of friends, and invite them to ask you questions. If you do not know the answer to a question, never guess or make up an answer or just say, "I don't know." Instead, you can say that you did not discover that answer during your research and then offer other information that you found of interest about the project. Be proud of the project and approach the judges with enthusiasm about your work.

CHECK IT OUT!

Read about your topic in many books and magazines. You are more likely to have a successful project if you are well informed about the topic. For the topics in this book, some tips are provided about specific places to look for information. Record in your journal all the information you find, and include for each source the author's name, the title of the book (or magazine name and article title), the numbers of the pages you read, where it was published, the publisher's name, and the year of publication.

1

Basic Parts

PROBLEM

What is a cell?

Materials

lemon gelatin dessert mix
1-quart (1-liter) resealable plastic bag
1-quart (1-liter) bowl
timer
large red grape
5 peanuts (with or without their
    shells)
adult helper

Procedure

1. Have your adult helper prepare the gelatin dessert mix according to the instructions on the box.

2. Allow the gelatin to cool to room temperature.

3. Pour the gelatin into the resealable bag and seal the bag. Place the bag in the bowl.

4. Place the bowl in the refrigerator to chill until the gelatin is firm (about 3 to 4 hours).

5. When the gelatin is firm, remove the bowl from the refrigerator and open the bag.

6. Use your fingers to insert the grape in the center of the gelatin. Insert the peanuts in the gelatin so that they are distributed evenly throughout the gelatin.

7. Reseal the bag and place it on a flat surface, such as the kitchen counter. Observe its shape.

8. Hold the bag over the bowl and gently squeeze the bag. Do not squeeze so hard that the bag opens. Observe the shape of the bag as you squeeze.

Results

You have made a model of the four common parts of all cells.

Why?

A **cell** is that part of any organism that is the smallest part that can exist on its own. (**Organisms** are all living things—people, plants, animals, and tiny living things called bacteria and fungi.) Cells differ in size and shape, but all have four common parts: a cell membrane, cytoplasm, mitochondria, and a nucleus. All four of these parts are represented in the model you made in this activity.

The plastic bag in your model represents the cell membrane. The **cell membrane** holds the cell together and protects the inner parts. The light-colored gelatin represents the grayish jellylike material, made mostly of water, called **cytoplasm** that fills the cell. Most of the chemical changes in the cell take place in the cytoplasm. (A **chemical change** is a change that produces one or more substances that are different from those present before the change.) The grape floating in the gelatin represents the nucleus. The **nucleus** is the control center that directs all the activities of the cell. The peanuts floating in the gelatin represent the "power stations" of the cell, called the **mitochondria**. In the mitochondria, food and **oxygen** (a gas in the air) combine to produce the energy needed for the cell to work and live.

The four common parts of a cell—cell membrane, cytoplasm, mitochondria, and nucleus—all work together and are necessary for the life of the cell. Like the basic model, many cells change shape when pressure is applied.

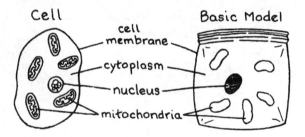

FOUR COMMON PARTS OF ALL CELLS

LET'S EXPLORE

1. How are plant cells different on the inside from other cells? One way is that most plant cells contain chloroplasts. **Chloroplasts** are green bodies

in plant cells that give plants their green color and in which food for the plant is made. Repeat the experiment, using 6 to 10 green grapes in addition to the red grape and peanuts. Insert the green grapes in the gelatin so that they are scattered throughout the gelatin. Do the grapes affect how the bag changes shape when at rest or when you squeeze it? Keep this model of the basic parts inside a plant cell for the next experiment.

2. Since plants do not have bones, what gives them support and shape? Set the cell model from the previous experiment in a small box, such as a shoe

box. Observe any change in the shape of the box as you place it on a flat surface or squeeze it. The box represents the stiff outer layer of a plant cell, called the **cell wall**. By placing the bag of gelatin, which represents the basic parts inside a plant cell, inside the box, you now have a basic model of a plant cell. **Science Fair Hint:** Place the plant cell model on a flat surface and take a photograph. Photograph the basic model of the four common parts of all cells from the original equipment on the same flat surface. Display these photos to demonstrate the support that a cell wall gives to a plant cell.

SHOW TIME!

1. **Specialized cells** are cells that perform a particular function, such as growth or absorbing water. A **tissue** is a group of specialized cells that perform a similar task. Demonstrate the difference between a plant cell and plant tissue by making five basic plant cell models, using the previous procedure. Put the lid on each box. Place two of the cell model boxes on top of two others to create two stacks, each two cells high. Place the fifth box near the two stacks. Fold 2 index cards in half. Label one card Plant Tissue and stand it in front of the two stacks. Label the other card Plant Cell and stand it in front of the fifth box. Display the boxes and photograph them. Use the photographs to prepare a poster to represent the difference between a plant cell and plant tissue.

2. **Organs** are structures consisting of different tissues grouped together to perform a specific function or functions. Plants have several organs. **Leaves** are special plant organs for manufacturing food. **Roots** and **stems** are special plant organs for **absorbing** (taking in) and **transporting** (carrying from one place to another) water, food, and minerals throughout the plant. Some plants have **flowers,** which contain organs for producing more plants. Find out more about these and other plant organs. Create and display a chart showing the different plant organs.

2

Spongy

PROBLEM

How does water move through moss?

Materials

1 tablespoon (15 ml)
tap water
sheet of typing paper
paper towel
2-inch (5-cm) section of dry sphag-
   num moss (available at a plant
   nursery or florist)
magnifying lens
timer
*NOTE: The section of moss should look
like a tiny leafy stem with roots.*

Procedure

1. Fill the spoon about one-fourth full
   with water.

2. Carefully set the spoon on the typing
   paper. Use the paper towel to blot up
   any water that spills onto the typing
   paper.

3. Place one end of the moss in the water
   in the spoon. Allow the other end to
   touch or hang above the paper.

4. Use the magnifying lens to observe
   the moss as often as possible for 30
   minutes. *NOTE: Keep the wet moss for
   the next experiment.*

Results

The moss slowly becomes wet, beginning with the end in the water. Finally,
water drips off the other end onto the
paper.

Why?

As water moves through moss, it is
distributed throughout the plant by a

process called diffusion. **Diffusion** is the spreading out of a material from a **concentrated** (to be crowded with a material) area to a less concentrated area.

The dry moss in this experiment acts like a sponge. It absorbs water from the spoon. The water moves from cell to cell as it diffuses throughout the plant.

Moss absorbs water this way because it is a nonvascular plant. There are two basic types of plants: vascular plants and nonvascular plants. **Vascular plants** have a **vascular system** that contains bundles of tubes called **vascular tubes**, which transport **sap** (a liquid containing water and minerals or food) throughout the plant. (See chapter 3, "Climbers," for more information about vascular plants.) **Nonvascular plants**, such as moss, do not contain a vascular system. Water, minerals, and food are transported through nonvascular plants by diffusion.

LET'S EXPLORE

Will water continue to move through wet moss? Repeat the experiment, using the wet moss from the original experiment. Add 1 drop of green food coloring to the water in the spoon. Note the color of the water moving through the moss and that of the water dripping onto the paper. **Science Fair Hint:** Take photos or make drawings of the moss every 5 to 10 minutes. Use them as part of a project display to represent the results of the experiment.

SHOW TIME!

1. To live, a plant on land must obtain and retain water, but it loses water through its outer surface. However, the outside of mosses and most plants is covered by a waxy film called the **cuticle**. The cuticle keeps a plant from losing too much water because it slows down the passage of **water vapor** (water in the gas state) through the plant's outer surface. Demonstrate the effect of the cuticle on water loss by dampening 2 paper towels with tap water. The towels should be wet but not dripping. Roll up one of the paper towels and lay it on a cookie sheet. Roll up the second paper towel in the same way, but wrap it with a piece of waxed paper about the size of the paper towel roll so that the outer surface of the towel is covered by the waxed paper. The waxed paper represents the cuticle covering a moss's epidermis. Secure the top and bottom of the waxed paper–covered towel with large paper clips, and place the covered towel on the cookie sheet. Set the

cookie sheet where it will receive direct sunlight. Unroll the towels after 12 hours and feel each.

2. Mosses grow best in shady areas and generally grow on the ground near and on the north side of trees. See for yourself that the north side of a tree has more shade. Find a tree that is not growing near other trees and buildings. Use a compass to determine the directions north, south, east, and west. Mark these directions by writing N, S, E, and W on separate index cards. Use tape to attach each card to a pencil, and insert each pencil in the ground around the tree in the appropriate place. Observe the tree as often as possible on a sunny day. Take photos or make sketches of the tree and its shadow during each observation.

3

Climbers

PROBLEM

How does water move through a leaf?

Materials

juice glass
tap water
red food coloring
scissors
large tree leaf, such as an oak leaf
crayons or colored markers
3 sheets of typing paper

Procedure

1. Fill the glass about one-fourth full with water.

2. Add enough food coloring to make the water a deep red color.

3. Use the scissors to cut across the end of the leaf's stem.

4. Stand the leaf in the glass of colored water.

5. Observe the leaf and make a colored drawing of it. Label the drawing Day 1.

6. Repeat step 5 at about the same time each day for the next 2 days. Label the drawings Day 2 and Day 3.

Results

The red color moves slowly through the leaf, first following the pattern made by the leaf's **veins** (the bundles of vascular tubes forming the framework through which liquids flow) and then throughout the rest of the leaf.

Why?

The leaf is part of a vascular plant. Like all vascular plants, the leaf has two main vascular tubes, xylem tubes and phloem tubes. **Xylem tubes** transport sap containing water and minerals upward from the roots through the plant. The xylem tubes also provide support for the plant because their walls are thick.

Phloem tubes transport sap containing water and food manufactured in the plant's leaves throughout the plant. In this activity, you saw the results of colored water moving through xylem tubes.

Scientists believe that **transpiration** (a process by which water vapor is lost through leaves) is responsible for the upward movement of water through xylem tubes against the pull of **gravity** (the force that pulls things toward the center of the earth). Xylem tubes from the roots to the leaves are believed to be filled with sap, which is mostly water. Some of the water in xylem tubes **evaporates** (changes from a liquid to a gas) during transpiration. As water is lost from the xylem tubes, the column of sap in the tube is pulled upward. This is because water **molecules** (the smallest particles of a substance that retain the properties of the substance) hold tightly to each other. As the water molecules in the xylem tubes move upward, water from the soil is pulled into the roots.

LET'S EXPLORE

1. Will water move the same way through a vascular plant that has a longer stem? Repeat the experiment, using a pale stalk of celery with pale leaves. (These can be found in the center of a celery bunch.)

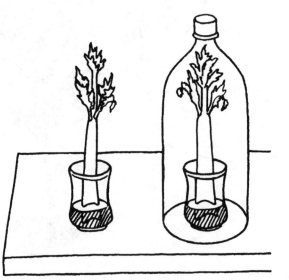

2. How do changes in the rate at which water evaporates from leaves affect the speed at which water moves through xylem tubes? Repeat the previous experiment, preparing 3 stalks of celery in 3 glasses. Ask an adult to cut the bottom from a 2-liter soda bottle. Cover one of the glasses with the bottle, as shown, and set the second glass next to the bottle. Set the third glass at a distance from the other glasses and in front of a blowing fan. *NOTE: A dry, windy environment increases evaporation.* Observe the celery stalks and leaves in each glass every 15 minutes for 1 hour and then as often as possible for 8 to 10 hours. **Science Fair Hint:** Display drawings of the results.

SHOW TIME!

1. Demonstrate transpiration by placing a clear plastic bag over a group of leaves at the end of a stem of a tree or bush. (Do not cut or break the stem off the plant.) Secure the bag to the stem by wrapping tape around the open end of the bag. Observe the contents of the bag as often as possible for 2 to 3 days.

2. As water moves into a cell, pressure builds up inside the cell. This internal pressure is called **turgor pressure**. The **turgidity** of a cell is its firmness due to turgor pressure. A decrease in turgidity causes plant stems to **wilt** (become limp). Demonstrate wilting by placing a fresh stalk of celery with high turgidity in an empty glass. Evaluate the turgidity of the celery by trying to bend the stalk. Test the turgidity again after 24 hours.

4

Reflectors

PROBLEM

Why are plant leaves green?

Materials

manila file folder
sheet of white typing paper
paper clip
flashlight
sheet of green construction paper or
   any bright green paper
ruler
helper

Procedure

1. Open the file folder slightly and stand it on a table.

2. Attach the white paper to one side of the standing folder with the paper clip. The white paper will be called the screen.

3. Lay the flashlight alongside the standing folder. Rotate the flashlight so that the lamp end faces away from the screen at a 45-degree (45°) angle.

4. Fold the green paper in half lengthwise (long end to long end) to make it easier to hold.

5. Hold the green paper about 4 inches (10 cm) from the lamp end of the flashlight.

6. Turn on the flashlight, then ask your helper to darken the room.

7. Observe the color of the screen.

Results

The screen looks green.

Why?

The screen looks green because of

something called pigment. **Pigments** are materials that absorb, reflect, and transmit visible light. **Visible light** is made up of colors of light that can be seen by the human eye, commonly

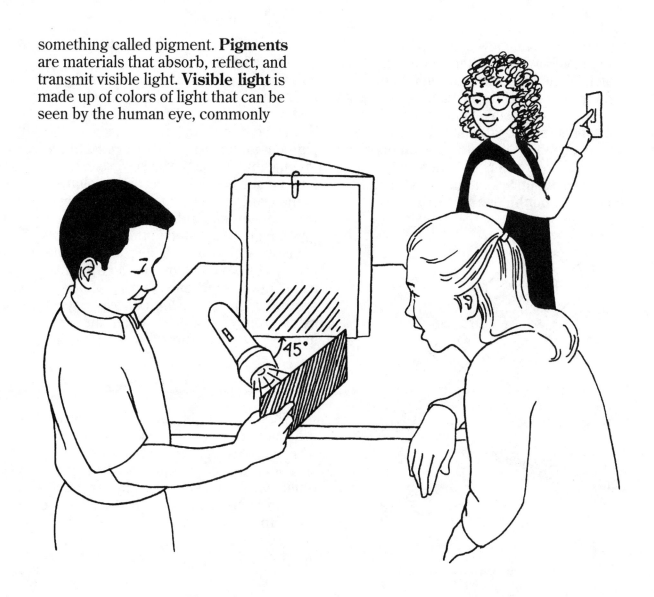

referred to as rainbow colors: red, orange, yellow, green, blue, indigo, and violet. White light, such as sunlight or light from a flashlight, is made up of the seven colors of visible light. When white light meets **matter** (the substance of which any object is made), any number of the different colors of light may be **reflected** (bounced back), **transmitted** (passed through), or absorbed.

When a pigment is illuminated, or brightened, with white light, the color you see is the color of light reflected and/or transmitted by the pigment. (The rest of the colors of light are absorbed.) You see green on the screen because the pigment in the colored paper reflects green light. Similarly, you see green when looking at a green leaf because a pigment in the leaf called chlorophyll reflects and transmits green light. **Chlorophyll** is a green pigment located in the chloroplasts of plants. Chlorophyll is necessary in the process by which plants produce food, called **photosynthesis**. During photosynthesis, plants use light energy trapped by chlorophyll to change water and a gas in the air called **carbon dioxide** into food.

LET'S EXPLORE

When white light strikes a red flower, the flower absorbs all the colors in the white light except red. The flower appears red because only red light is reflected. Demonstrate this by repeating the experiment, using red paper. **Science Fair Hint:** Construct and use a diagram like the one shown as part of a project display.

SHOW TIME!

The colors of light that materials such as pigment absorb and transmit can be determined by an instrument called a **spectrophotometer**. Make a simple spectrophotometer by laying a sheet of white paper on a table. The sheet of paper will be your screen. Prepare a liquid containing pigment from a leaf, such as a geranium leaf, by tearing the leaf into small pieces and placing them in a clear plastic cup. Add 3 tablespoons (45 ml) of rubbing alcohol to the cup. *CAUTION: Keep the alcohol away from your nose and mouth.* Stir the contents of the cup as often as possible for 1 hour, then remove the pieces of leaf.

Hold the cup about 4 inches (10 cm) above the screen, and the flashlight about 2 inches (5 cm) above the cup. Shine the light through the liquid in the cup and onto the screen. The color seen on the screen is the color transmitted by the pigment removed from the leaf. The colors absorbed are all the colors making up white light, minus the transmitted and any reflected colors. Take a color photograph or make a color diagram to represent the results. Find out how professional spectrophotometers work.

CHECK IT OUT!

There are three groups of pigment in plants: chlorophyll, carotenoids, and phycobilins. Find out more about these pigments. Which colors does each group absorb, reflect, and transmit?

5

Lights Out!

PROBLEM

Why does green grass turn yellow?

Materials

medium-size cooking pot or metal
   bowl
area of short grass
1 quart (1 liter) water (optional)

Procedure

*NOTE: This experiment causes tempo-
rary yellow patches on the grass. You must
get an adult's approval to perform the
experiment.*

1. Place the pot, open end down, on an
   area of green grass. *NOTE: If the soil
   is very dry, pour the water over the
   grass before placing the pot on it.*

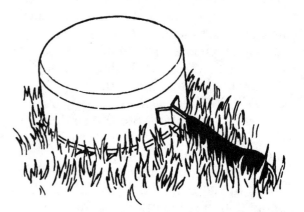

2. Allow the pot to sit undisturbed for 10
   days.

3. At the end of 10 days, remove the pot.
   Compare the color of the grass that
   was beneath the pot with the color of
   the grass around the area that was
   covered.

Results

After 10 days, the grass covered by the pot has turned from green to yellow. The grass around the covered area remains green.

Why?

Plants like grass are green because there is chlorophyll in their chloroplasts. Light is necessary for chlorophyll to develop in the chloroplasts. Without light, chemical changes in the chloroplasts cause chlorophyll to break down faster than it is made. The chloroplasts contain mainly chlorophyll, but they also contain other pigments, such as pale yellow pigments called **xanthophylls** and yellow or orange pigments called **carotenes**. When chlorophyll breaks down, the yellow pigments in the grass, like those in any plant, are exposed, and the plant looks yellow. The loss of green color in plants is called **chlorosis**.

LET'S EXPLORE

1. Does the amount of air received by the covered grass affect the results? Repeat the experiment, using 2 more pots. One pot should be deeper and the other pot shallower. **Science Fair Hint:** Take color photographs of the grassy area under each pot at the beginning and end of the experiment. Display the photographs to represent the results.

2. At what rate does the chlorophyll in grass break down? You can determine a general rate by observing color changes over a measured time period. Repeat the original experiment, using 10 small containers, such as empty cans. Push the cans into the soil or place heavy objects, such as bricks or rocks, on top of the cans to prevent the wind from blowing them over. Place the cans in position at night so that the experiment begins at sunrise on the next day.

   Late in the afternoon of the first day, while there is still enough light to see the grass, remove one of the cans and take a color photograph of the grass the can covered, plus some of the grass that surrounded the can. At the same time on the second day, repeat the procedure with the second can. Continue to remove a can and make a photograph at the same time each day for 10 days. Compare the photographs to determine how long it takes for the color of the grass to change noticeably. *NOTE: The amount of sunlight can vary from week to week. If possible, repeat this experiment during a later week and compare the results.*

SHOW TIME!

Try another way to determine the rate at which chlorophyll breaks down. Cut twenty ½-by-1-inch (1.25-by-2.5-cm) strips from a sheet of black construction paper. At sunset on the night before you begin the experiment, fold each strip in half, wrap it around a blade of grass, and secure it with a small paper clip. Use the weather report in your local newspaper or on TV to determine how many hours of daylight are predicted for the next day.

On the first day of the experiment, after the grass has received half of the light predicted for that day, remove one black strip from one blade of grass. Cut the blade of grass off the plant and tape it to a sheet of white paper. Label the paper Day 1 (Half Day) and photograph the page. At sunset on the first day, remove a second black strip from a second blade of grass. Again cut off the blade of grass and tape it to a sheet of white paper. Label the paper Day 1 (Full Day) and photograph the page. Repeat this procedure every day for 10 days. Display the photographs to represent the results.

CHECK IT OUT!

In the autumn, green leaves turn different colors, such as red and yellow. Find out more about the color of fall leaves. Use a biology text and/or an encyclopedia to find out more about this color change. How does temperature affect the change? What color is the pigment anthocyanin?

6

Bloomers

PROBLEM

What are the parts of a flower?

Materials

sheet of tracing paper
pencil
scissors
3 sheets of construction paper: 2
    green, 1 red
walnut-size ball of modeling clay
flexible straw (use a green one if avail-
    able)
transparent tape
one-hole paper punch
ruler
six 3-inch (7.5-cm) -long pipe cleaners:
    1 green, 5 yellow
¼ teaspoon (1.25 l) fine-ground yellow
    cornmeal

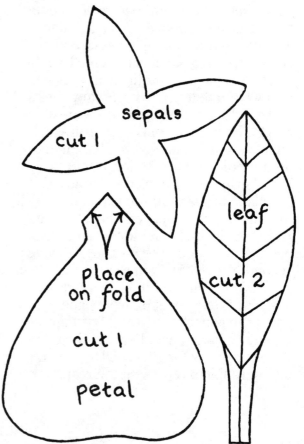

Procedure

1. Lay the tracing paper over the patterns for the petal, sepals, and leaf. Trace and cut out the 3 patterns.

2. Use the leaf and sepals patterns to cut one sepal and two petals from one of the sheets of green construction paper.

3. Fold the red construction paper in half twice. Place the petal pattern on the folded paper as shown. Draw around the petal pattern, then cut along the lines you drew. Unfold the paper.

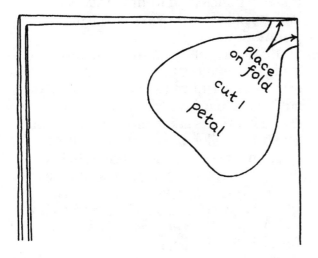

4. Place the second sheet of green paper on a table. Use the clay to stand the straw on the paper, flexible end up. Tape the leaves to the lower part of the straw.

5. Slightly bend about ½ inch (1.25 cm) of one end of the green pipe cleaner and insert the bent end in the end of the straw.

6. Make a hole in the center of the sepals and petals with the paper punch.

7. Insert the sepals over the green pipe cleaner through the hole in the sepals. Do the same for the petals.

8. Bend ½ inch (2.5 cm) of one end of a yellow pipe cleaner to a 90° angle. Insert the straight end of the yellow pipe cleaner through the holes in the petals and sepals and into the straw.

9. Repeat step 8 for each yellow pipe cleaner. Sprinkle the cornmeal over the bent ends of the yellow pipe cleaners.

   NOTE: Keep the flower model for the next experiment.

Results

You have made a three-dimensional model of a flower that shows its basic parts.

Why?

There are two types of plants: plants that flower and plants that do not flower. Flowers contain **reproductive organs** (organs that produce more plants). Flowering plants reproduce when two special cells, a female **egg** and a male **sperm**, join together. This joining, called **fertilization**, results in the formation of a seed.

In your model, the green pipe cleaner represents the top of the **pistil** (the female reproductive organ), and the yellow pipe cleaners represent **stamens** (the male reproductive organ). The pistil, which contains the eggs, is in the center of the flower and surrounded by several stamens. The stamens produce **pollen grains**, yellow dustlike grains that contain sperm, represented by cornmeal in your model. For fertilization to occur, pollen grains must be transferred from the stamens to the pistil. This process is called **pollination**.

Petals are often brightly colored leaflike structures that surround and protect the pistil and stamens. A sugary liquid substance called **nectar** is produced in organs at the base of the petals. The bright color and the nectar attract birds and insects. Pollen grains stick to the bodies of birds and insects and are carried from one flower to the next, which helps pollination occur. **Sepals** are leaflike, usually green, and surround the flower before it opens.

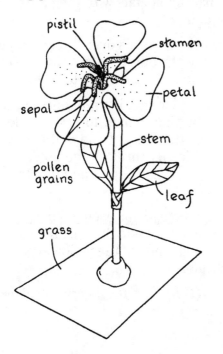

LET'S EXPLORE

Most flowers have the same general structure. A **complete flower** contains a pistil, stamens, petals, and sepals, and an **incomplete flower** is missing one or more of these flower parts. Repeat the experiment twice, first preparing an incomplete flower by leaving off the petals, then preparing a second incomplete flower by leaving off the sepals and petals. **Science Fair Hint:** Fold 2 index cards in half to use as identification cards. Label one card Complete Flower and the other card Incomplete Flower. Display the two models of incomplete flowers and the model of the complete flower from the original experiment. Find out whether a flower can lack both male and female reproductive organs (stamens and pistil).

SHOW TIME!

Angiosperms are flowering plants that have a vascular system. They are divided into two groups, **monocotyledons** or **monocots** and **dicotyledons** or **dicots**. (For more information about these two groups, see chapter 13, "Single.") These two groups have different numbers of flower parts, such as petals, sepals, and stamens. In monocots, these flower parts usually occur in multiples of three. In dicots, the parts usually occur in multiples of four or five. Observe flowers and identify types from the two angiosperm groups. Take photos, make drawings, or follow instructions from a crafts book on preserving flowers to prepare a display showing flowers of monocots and dicots.

7

Enlarged

PROBLEM

How do plants make seeds and fruit?

Materials?

2 sheets of white typing paper
pen
scissors
transparent tape
ruler
manila file folder

Procedure

1. On one sheet of typing paper, draw and label a flower pistil as shown in the first diagram.

2. Cut out the section of the pistil indicated by the dotted line in the diagram.

3. Tape the second sheet of typing paper behind the first sheet. As shown in the

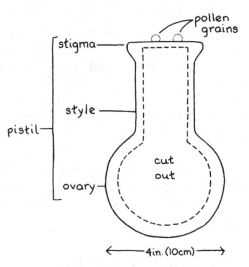

second diagram, do not place tape directly above or below the pistil.

4. Drawing on the second sheet of paper within the cutout section of the first sheet, use the diagram to draw and label the inner parts of the pistil.

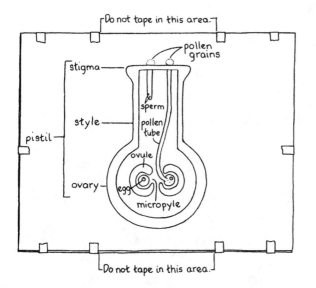

Do not tape in this area.

pollen grains

stigma

sperm

style

pollen tube

pistil

ovule

ovary

egg

micropyle

Do not tape in this area.

5. Cut a 4-by-10-inch (10-by-25-cm) strip from the file folder. Insert the strip between the two sheets of paper in the untaped area so that the strip covers the drawing in the cutout.

6. Slowly pull the paper strip down.

Results

As you pull the paper strip down, the pollen tubes appear to grow, and one tube reaches the lower part of the pistil.

Why?

The pistil (the female reproductive organ inside a flower of an angiosperm) has three basic parts: the stigma, the style, and the ovary. The **stigma** is the sticky top that holds pollen grains that land on it. The **style** is a tubelike structure that supports the stigma and connects it with the rounded base of the pistil, called the **ovary**.

Inside the ovary are seedlike parts called **ovules,** which contain eggs. The ovules ripen into **seeds** as a result of fertilization of the eggs by sperm. Sperm are contained in pollen grains. Pollination occurs when the pollen grains from the stamen land on the stigma.

After pollination, the pollen grains begin to grow a long tube down the style toward the eggs. Each tube, called a **pollen tube**, contains two sperm. The tube enters the ovule through a hole in the ovule wall called the **micropyle**. As soon as the tube comes in contact with the egg, the two sperm are released. One sperm fertilizes the egg, producing a **zygote** (a fertilized egg) that develops into an **embryo** (an organism in its earliest stages of development). The other

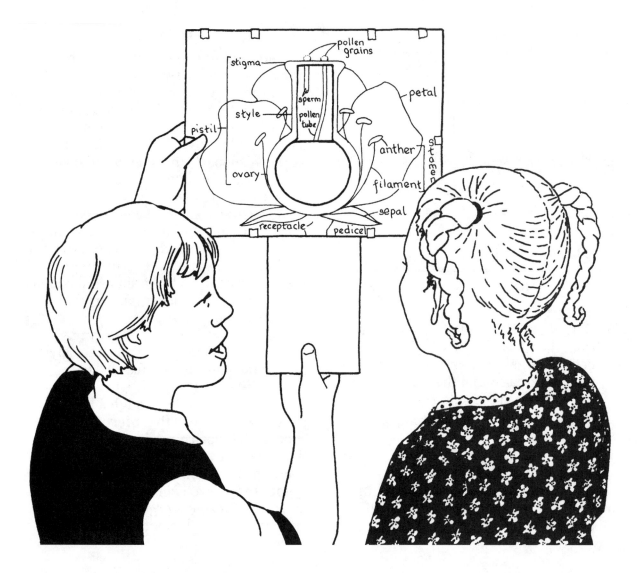

sperm combines with a special cell to form the **endosperm** (the nourishing tissue for the developing embryo).

After fertilization, the sepals, petals, and stamens wither and the ovary and ovules develop. The ovules develop into the seeds of the plant, each of which contains an embryo and a stored food supply. In flowering plants, the seed is enclosed in a **fruit** (enlarged ovary). In many plants the **receptacle** (the top of the flower stem supporting the reproductive organs) also enlarges and becomes part of the fruit.

LET'S EXPLORE

Use a biology book and information in chapter 6, "Bloomers," to find out about the other parts of a flower. Draw the rest of the flower around the pistil on the model of the pistil from the original experiment. Label each part. **Science Fair Hint:** Display the model as part of your project and use it when giving an oral presentation.

SHOW TIME!

1. Observe the outside of the apple and find the stem and the dried stamens

opposite the stem. Ask an adult to cut an apple in half from the stamens to the stem. Make and display a diagram similar to the one shown, comparing the fruit parts to the flower parts.

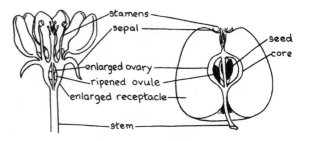

2. Fruits help to scatter seeds as well as protect them. Some fruits, such as beggar-ticks, have stickers or spines on them. These stickers catch on clothes or the fur of animals, which carries the fruit with its seeds away from the parent plant. The process by which seeds are scattered is called **seed dispersal.** Find out more about seed dispersal. How are seeds of fleshy fruits, such as apples or berries, dispersed? Prepare a seed dispersal display with examples of seeds for each type of dispersal.

8

Hidden

PROBLEM

Where are the seeds in a pinecone?

Materials

several sheets of newspaper
2 old washcloths
3 to 5 immature pinecones (small
    pinecones with tightly closed scales)
timer (optional)
adult helper

Procedure

1. Spread out the newspaper on a table.

2. Wrap a washcloth around each end of one of the pinecones.

3. Holding a washcloth-covered end in each hand, twist the cone back and forth several times to loosen its scales. *NOTE: If it is too difficult to*

twist the cone, soak all of the cones in water for 2 to 3 hours. Ask an adult for help if it is still too difficult to twist the cone.

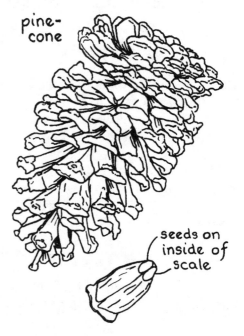

pine-
cone

seeds on
inside of
scale

4. While holding the base of the cone with the cloth, use the fingers of your other hand to pull out several scales near the tip of the cone.

5. Look for two seeds on the inside of each scale, as shown. *NOTE: If you do not find seeds, repeat steps 2 to 4 with another pinecone.*

Results

Two seeds, each attached to a paperlike wing, are found on the inside of the scales of the pinecone.

Why?

The pinecone contains the seeds of a pine tree. Pine trees are **conifers**, nonflowering plants that reproduce by forming cones. Most conifers are **evergreen** (having leaves that remain green all through the year) trees with small needle-shaped leaves and two types of cones. One is a small cone, called the **pollen cone**, which contains pollen and forms in groups at the tip of a branch. The other is a **seed cone**, which contains seeds and usually forms as a single cone away from the tip of a branch.

In the spring, wind blows pollen grains from the pollen cones to the seed cones. The pollen grains form sperm that fertilize the eggs at the base of the seed cone's scales. Each fertilized egg develops into a plant embryo, which is part of the seed. It can take two or more years for the seeds to develop completely. During the seed development stage, the cone grows larger, and the scales close tightly to protect the seeds.

LET'S EXPLORE

Are seeds found only inside the scales at the tip of the cone? Repeat the experiment, examining scales from tip to base. **Science Fair Hint:** Pull the scales out far enough to see the seeds, then photograph the cone. Use the photo as part of a project display.

SHOW TIME!

1. When the seeds have completely developed, the scales of pinecones open slightly and the seeds fall to the ground or are blown by the wind. Low **humidity** (wetness of the air) causes the cones to dry. Demonstrate the effect that drying has on the opening or closing of the cone scales. Have an adult heat cones to dry them. Line a cake pan with aluminum foil. Place 4 to 6 pinecones in the pan. Half of the cones should have open scales and half should have closed scales. Have an adult put the pan in an oven set to low and bake the cones for 30 minutes. After 30 minutes, have the adult remove the cones from the oven.

When the cones have cooled, observe the position of the scales. *NOTE: Save the pinecones for the next experiment.*

2. Determine the effect that rain and/or high humidity have on pinecone scales. Place one of the pinecones from the previous experiment in a glass of water. Observe the position of the cone's scales as often as possible for 30 to 45 minutes. Repeat, using the other pinecones. Take photographs of the cones before and after you soak them, and display the photos to represent the results.

CHECK IT OUT!

Conifers are *gymnosperms*, which are nonflowering plants with seeds. Their seeds are uncovered, meaning they are not found inside fruits but in cones. Use a biology text to find out more about the reproduction of gymnosperms. What are male and female gametophytes? What is a sporophyte? Use the information to prepare a display chart representing stages of the life cycle of a gymnosperm, such as a pine tree.

9

Inside and Out

PROBLEM

What's on the outside of a pinto bean?

Materials

4 to 5 dry pinto beans
coffee cup
ruler
tap water
timer
paper towel

Procedure

1. Place the beans in the cup and cover them with about 2 inches (5 cm) of water.

2. Soak the beans for 24 hours.

3. After 24 hours, take the beans out of the cup and place them on the paper towel to absorb the excess water.

4. Inspect the outside of the beans. Use your fingernails to remove and examine part of the outer covering from one of the beans.

NOTE: Keep the remaining beans for the next two experiments.

Results

The outside of the bean consists of (1) a brown outer coating, (2) a light-colored, oval-shaped scar, and (3) a small dot at one end of the scar. The outer covering is thin and peels off easily.

Why?

Beans are angiosperm seeds. The outer covering of a seed, called the **seed coat**, is formed by the wall of an ovule. The seed coat helps protect the inside of the seed from insects, disease, and damage. The scar on the seed coat is the **hilum** (the place where the ovary was attached to the ovule). The small dot at one end of the hilum is the **micropyle.**

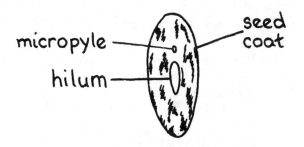

LET'S EXPLORE

1. What's under the seed coat of a pinto bean? Use one of the soaked pinto beans from the experiment. Remove the seed coat to reveal a white structure with two separate halves connected at a single spot at the top. The two halves are **cotyledons**, or seed leaves, which are simple leaves that store food for the developing plant embryo. Extending from the connecting spot is a beak-shaped structure called the **hypocotyl**. The hypocotyl is the part of the plant embryo that

develops into the lower stem and root. The tip of the hypocotyl, called the **radicle**, develops into roots. Use a magnifying lens to examine these parts. Repeat the procedure, using 3 or 4 more beans.

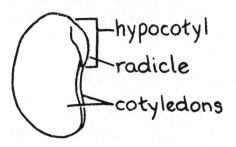

2. What's inside a pinto bean? Use the soaked beans from the original experiment. Remove the seed coat and gently pry the cotyledons open with your fingernail, then spread them apart. Be careful not to break the hypocotyl. Use a magnifying lens to study the parts of the embryo inside. Use the diagram to identify the following parts of the **embryonic** (undeveloped) **shoot** (part of a plant that grows above the ground).

- **epicotyl:** The part of a plant embryo, located above the hypocotyl, that develops into the plant's stem, leaves, flowers, and fruit.
- **plumule:** The embryonic shoot tip that consists of several tiny, immature leaves that at maturity form the first true leaves.

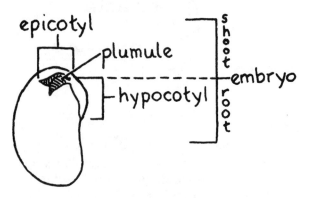

Science Fair Hint: Prepare and display a labeled drawing of the outside and inside of the bean.

3. What's inside other beans? Repeat the previous experiment, using different beans, such as lima and kidney.

SHOW TIME!

Which part of the embryo in a pinto bean develops first? Soak 30 to 40 beans in 1 cup (250 ml) of water. *NOTE: You'll need the extra beans in case some of the embryos are damaged.* Fold a paper towel in half twice and place it on a piece of aluminum foil that is about 12 inches (30 cm) square. Wet the towel with water. Place all but 3 of the soaked beans on the wet paper towel. Fold the aluminum foil over the beans to keep them moist. Open the 3 reserved beans and use a magnifying lens to observe their embryo parts. Make one diagram showing a cotyledon and the attached embryo. The diagram should indicate the size of the cotyledon and the embryo parts. Each day for 7 days, remove 3 beans from the foil and observe their embryos. Make another diagram showing size and location of the embryo in the cotyledon. Create and display a poster using the drawings to show the development of the bean embryo.

CHECK IT OUT!

The seed coats of different seeds vary in color, thickness, and texture.

Sometimes the seed coat is smooth and paper-thin, like that of a pinto bean. A coconut's seed coat, however, is rough, thick, and hard. A seed cannot develop into a plant until the seed coat is broken.

Find out how the seed coats of different seeds are broken. For more information about the breaking of seed coats, see chapter 10, "Attractive."

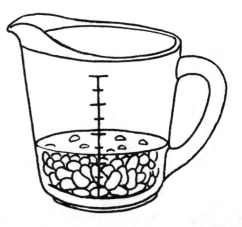

Attractive

PROBLEM

How does water affect pinto beans?

Materials

½ cup (125 ml) dry pinto beans
clear plastic 2-cup (500-ml) measuring
    cup
tap water
timer

Procedure

1. Place the beans in the cup.

2. Add enough water to the cup to cover
   the beans.

3. Observe and record the **volume**
   (amount of space taken up) of the
   beans in the cup.

4. Allow the beans to sit undisturbed for
   24 hours.

5. After 24 hours, observe and record
   the volume of the beans. Discard the
   beans.

Results

After 24 hours, the volume of the
beans has increased. Little or no water is
left in the cup.

Why?

The volume of the beans increases while the volume of water decreases because the water moves into the beans. The beans are **hydrophilic**, meaning they have an attraction for water. The beans are also **porous**, meaning water can pass through them. The process by which a hydrophilic, porous material absorbs water is called **imbibition**. When dry seeds, such as the beans, are watered, they **imbibe** (absorb) water and swell.

LET'S EXPLORE

1a. How would excessive amounts of water affect the bean? Repeat the experiment, filling the cup with water.

b. Do the beans imbibe water at a constant rate? Repeat the previous experiment. Record the volume of the beans on a chart similar to the one shown every 2 hours for 12 hours. Then record again once 24 hours after the experiment began, and once again 48 hours afterward. **Science Fair Hint:** Prepare and use a graph comparing the time and volume of the beans as part of a project display.

2. Are other beans as hydrophilic as pinto beans? Repeat the experiment, using a different type of bean, such as lima beans. Compare the rate of change in volume of the different type of bean to the rate of change in volume of the pinto beans in order to determine which is more hydrophilic.

Time (hours)

		0	2	4	6	8	10	12	24	48
Volume	cups	½								
	ml	125								

SHOW TIME!

1. How does imbibition affect the seed coat of a bean? Begin by recording the appearance of the seed coats of 2 dry pinto beans. Then, determine the hardness of the seed coats of the beans by scratching your fingernail across the seed coats. Place 12 beans in ½ cup (125 ml) of water. Three times daily for two days, remove 2 of the beans from the water and observe the appearance and hardness of their seed coats.

2. Would pressure on the beans affect imbibition? Use fifteen 10-ounce (300-ml) clear plastic cups. Fill 5 of the cups with pinto beans to a level of 1 inch (2.5 cm). Place a strip of masking tape down the side of each bean-filled cup. Mark the level of the beans on the tape. Cover the beans with about 1 inch (2.5 cm) of water.

   Fill the remaining 10 cups three-fourths full with sand. Place a sand-filled cup inside each of 4 bean-filled cups. The bottom of each sand-filled cup must rest on top of the beans. Stack the remaining sand-filled cups as shown. Mark the level of the beans every 2 hours for 12 hours. At the end of 12 hours, remove the sand-filled cups. Make a chart recording the level of the beans in each cup at each observation. Display the charted results.

cup1 cup2 cup3 cup4 cup5

11

Getting Started

PROBLEM

How long does it take a pinto bean to begin growing?

Materials

paper towels
10-ounce (300-ml) clear plastic cup
6 pinto beans
tap water
magnifying lens

Procedure

1. Fold a paper towel in half and use it to line the inside of the cup.

2. Crumple several paper towels together and stuff them into the cup.

Use enough towels to hold the paper lining firmly in place around the inside of the cup.

3. Place the beans between the cup and the lining, spacing the beans evenly around the **perimeter** (the measurement of a boundary) of the cup.

4. Moisten the paper towels in the cup with water. Keep the paper towels in the cup moist, but not dripping wet, during the entire experiment.

5. Use the magnifying lens to observe the beans two or three times daily until growth is observed. This will occur within 4 to 5 days.

Results

The first sign of growth is the breaking of the seed coat of the bean and the hypocotyl pushing through.

Why?

One way that plants **propagate** (produce new organisms) is by seeds. The process by which a seed **sprouts** (begins to grow) or develops is called **germination**. At the start of germination, the embryo does not begin life, but rather resumes growth that stopped when the seed matured. In the experiments in this book, the time it takes from planting a seed to the first signs of growth is called **germination starting time** (GST).

LET'S EXPLORE

1. Do **nutrients** (materials needed for the life and growth of living organisms) affect GST? Repeat the experiment, preparing 2 cups of beans. Wet the paper towels in one cup with distilled water and those in the other cup with a liquid commercial plant fertilizer. Prepare the fertilizer by doubling the water in the instructions on the package.

2. Is GST the same for all seeds? Repeat the original experiment, using different kinds of seeds, such as peas, squash, or zinnia seeds. **Science Fair Hint:** Use drawings or photos of each seed type to create a display that represents the GST results for each.

3. Does light affect GST? Repeat the original experiment, preparing 2 cups of beans. Cover one of the cups with a sheet of black construction paper wrapped around the cup. Fold and staple the top and sides of the paper.

Observe the beans two to three times a day until the first signs of growth are seen. Lift the paper covering to observe the beans in the covered cup.

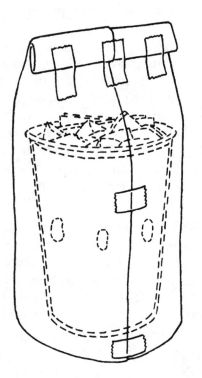

SHOW TIME!

In this book, the time it takes from planting a seed to the end of germination is called **germination time** (GT). GT is determined by the time it takes for the epicotyl to fully emerge from the cotyledons. Does the depth the seed is planted affect GT? Place a piece of masking tape down the side of 3 cups. Label the cups 1, 2, and 3. Place 2 seeds in the bottom of cup 1. Fill cup 2 about one-fourth full with soil, and place 2 beans on the surface of the soil. Fill cup 3 about one-half full with soil, and place 2 beans on the soil. Fill each cup three-fourths full with soil. The height of the soil in each cup must be the same. Keep the soil moist throughout the experiment.

CHECK IT OUT!

Seeds remain *dormant* (inactive) until certain conditions exist. For example, the seeds of some desert plants contain chemicals that prevent germination. The seeds are able to grow only after sufficient rainfall washes out these chemicals. Find out more about the conditions for breaking the dormancy of different seeds.

12

Double

PROBLEM

How does a pinto bean seedling develop?

Materials

paper towels
10-ounce (300-ml) clear plastic cup
6 dry pinto beans
tap water

Procedure

1. Fold a paper towel in half and use it to line the inside of the cup.

2. Crumple several paper towels together and stuff them into the cup. Use enough towels to hold the paper lining firmly in place around the inside of the cup.

3. Place the beans between the cup and the paper lining, spacing the beans evenly around the perimeter of the cup.

4. Moisten the paper towels in the cup with water. Keep the paper towels in the cup moist, but not dripping wet, during the entire experiment.

5. Observe the beans each day for 21 days.

Results

The seed coat breaks and the hypocotyl emerges. The free end of the hypocotyl grows down, and the end attached to the cotyledons grows up. The attached end is bent, but in time

straightens and raises the cotyledons. Later, a stem and leaves grow above the cotyledons and the cotyledons wither and fall away.

Why?

As a pinto bean or any angiosperm seed germinates, two systems, root and shoot, develop. The **root system** is **subterranean** (below ground) and consists of many branching roots. The **shoot system** is **aerial** (above ground) and consists of a shoot.

During germination, the parts of the bean (described in chapter 9, "Inside and Out") begin to grow. The end of the hypocotyl, the radicle, is the first part to emerge, grows downward, and eventually develops into the root system.

The hypocotyl lengthens, forming a hook at the end attached to the cotyledons. As the hooked hypocotyl grows upward, it would cut a passage through the soil if the bean were planted. This allows the attached cotyledons and epicotyl to be pulled through the soil without injury. After breaking through the soil, the hypocotyl straightens and raises the cotyledons and epicotyl upward. The epicotyl develops into the shoot, which at maturity consists of stems, leaves, flowers, and fruits. At first, two tiny leaves, which are the first true leaves, develop. Up to this point, the **seedling** (a young plant grown from a seed) has gotten its nutrients from the cotyledons, but now in the presence of light, chlorophyll is manufactured in the leaves and used to produce food. As the food supply in the cotyledons is used up, the cotyledons wither and fall away.

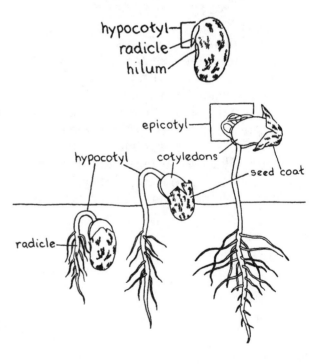

LET'S EXPLORE

What is the rate of growth for the hypocotyl? Repeat the experiment. At the first appearance of the hypocotyl, record the length of the hypocotyl as zero. Then, record the length of the hypocotyl at the same time each day for 7 days. **Science Fair Hint:** Prepare and display a graph of the growth rate.

SHOW TIME!

1. Would planting the beans in soil affect the results? Fill a clear plastic cup three-fourths full with potting soil. Plant 6 beans about ½ inch (1.25 cm) beneath the surface of the soil so that they are visible through the side of the cup. Keep the soil moist with water. Observe the cup every day for 21 days. **Science Fair Hint:** When observing the beans, take photographs to use as part of a project display to represent the results.

2. Do other dicots develop the way pinto beans do? Repeat the previous experiment, using 2 cups. Plant 6 lima beans in one cup and 6 peas in the other cup. During development, observe and record the position of the cotyledons, the length of the hypocotyl, and the length of the epicotyl of each seed. Then, make a comparison of beans and peas.

CHECK IT OUT!

Plant hormones are chemicals that control plant growth and development. Use biology texts and encyclopedias to find out more about these chemicals. What effect do auxins have on seedling growth? How do gibberellins affect germination?

13

Single

PROBLEM

What are the first signs of corn seed germination?

Materials

paper towels
10-ounce (300-ml) clear plastic cup
6 corn kernels (available in a plant
   nursery, feed store, or seed catalog)
tap water
magnifying lens

Procedure

1. Fold a paper towel in half and use it to line the inside of the cup.

2. Crumple several paper towels together and stuff them into the cup. Use enough towels to hold the paper lining firmly in place around the inside of the cup.

3. Place the corn kernels between the cup and the paper lining, spacing the kernels evenly around the perimeter of the cup.

4. Moisten the paper towels in the cup with water. Keep the paper towels in the cup moist, but not dripping wet, during the entire experiment.

5. Use the magnifying lens to observe the kernels each day for 7 days or until two tubelike structures appear on the outside of each kernel,

whichever comes first.

NOTE: Keep the cup of corn kernels for the next experiment.

Results

Two tubelike structures grow out of each kernel in opposite directions.

Why?

A corn kernel is a fruit. The corn seed is inside the fruit, but the kernel is often called a corn seed. Corn seeds are monocots, or monocotyledon seeds, because they contain a single cotyledon. Unlike dicots, most monocots store the food supply for the growing embryo in the endosperm surrounding the cotyledon rather than in the cotyledon. The cotyledon is very thin and absorbs the nutrients stored in the endosperm during germination.

Before germination, the embryo inside the corn seed is enclosed in a protective covering. The top part, called the **coleoptile**, covers the plumule, and the bottom part, called the **coleorhiza**, covers the radicle. When the corn seed germinates, the coleorhiza breaks through the seed coat and begins to grow downward. The coleoptile also breaks through the seed coat, but it grows upward, in the opposite direction of the coleorhiza.

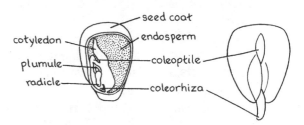

LET'S EXPLORE

As a corn seed germinates, the tip of its plumule grows upward and breaks through the end of the coleoptile. The tip of its radicle grows downward and breaks through the end of the coleorhiza. Do these parts of the embryo break through their protective coverings at the same time? Allow the cup of developing corn seeds from the original experiment to continue to grow until the plumule and/or radicle is seen. Use the magnifying lens to observe the tips of the coleoptile and coleorhiza. **Science Fair Hint:** Make drawings of the corn seeds' daily development to use as part of a project display.

Show Time!

1. In dicots, such as pinto beans, a hook in the hypocotyl pushes through the ground and straightens to pull the tender tip of the plumule upward. (See chapter 12, "Double," for more information about this protective hook.) In monocots, such as corn seeds, the coleoptile covers the plumule. Do monocots also have a hook? Fold a paper towel in half twice and lay it on a 12-inch (30-cm-square) piece of aluminum foil. Place 6 corn kernels and 6 pinto beans on one side of the folded towel. Moisten the towel with water. Fold the towel over the corn kernels and beans, then wrap the aluminum foil over the towel. Unfold the foil daily for 7 days and observe the development of the coleoptile of each corn seed. Compare the growth of the coleoptile to the growth of the hypocotyl in the beans. Take photographs of the daily development of the beans and corn seeds and display the photos to represent the results.

2a. The basic difference between monocots and dicots is the number of their cotyledons, but there are other differences, such as their leaves, stems, roots, and flowers. Examine some of the differences between monocots and dicots by growing both types of seedlings. Fill 2 plastic cups three-fourths full with potting soil. Plant 6 corn kernels in one cup and 6 pinto beans in the other cup. Each seed should be about ½ inch (1.25 cm) beneath the surface of the soil so that it is visible through the side of the cup. Moisten the soil with water and keep it moist during the experiment. Allow the plants to grow for 3 weeks or until fully developed leaves form.

   Compare the stems and root systems of the corn and bean plants. What differences do you notice? Compare the shapes of the leaves of the two plants. Make a rubbing of each leaf type by placing each leaf under a sheet of typing paper and rubbing the side of a

crayon across the paper until a print of the leaf appears. Use the leaf rubbings as part of a project display.

b. To show the differences between monocot and dicot plants, create a display by pressing the leaves, stems, and roots of an entire corn plant and bean plant from the previous experiment. For information about pressing plants, see page 53 in *Janice VanCleave's Science Fair Projects* (also published by Wiley).

14

Dividers

PROBLEM

How do pinto bean plant stems grow?

Materials

9-ounce (270-ml) paper cup
potting soil
pencil
4 dry pinto beans
ruler
saucer
tap water
marking pen

Procedure

1. Fill the cup about three-fourths full with potting soil.

2. Use the pencil to punch four to six holes around the perimeter of the bottom edge of the cup.

3. Plant the beans in the soil by pushing them into the soil about ½ inch (1.25 cm) below the surface.

4. Place the cup in the saucer and moisten the soil with water.

5. Allow the seeds to germinate and the seedlings to grow to a height of about 6 inches (15 cm) above the rim of the cup. This will take 14 or more days.

6. Wait until the seedlings have grown 6 inches (15 cm) above the rim of the cup. Then use the marking pen to mark two equal sections on the stem of each plant between the true leaves and cotyledons.

7. Measure and record the length of the two sections between the marks: section 1, between the true leaves and the center mark, and section 2, between the center mark and the cotyledons.

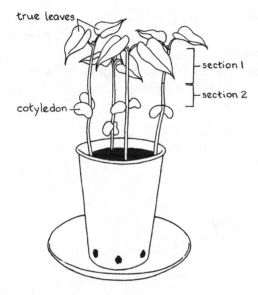

true leaves

section 1

section 2

cotyledon

8. At the same time each day for 14 days, measure and record the length of each section.

Results

The only (or greatest) change in growth occurs in section 1.

Why?

Plant stems **elongate** (grow longer) mainly in one area, called the meristem. The **meristem** is plant tissue made up of **meristematic cells**, which divide and produce other, similar cells. This process of cell division is called **mitosis**. In mitosis, the cell parts duplicate themselves and then divide into two separate cells. Stems grow as their meristematic cells duplicate and divide. As shown in this experiment, the bean plant grew only or mostly in the upper section of the stem, which means that meristematic cells are located in this area.

LET'S EXPLORE

1. Is the rate of growth the same during the day as during the night? Repeat the experiment, measuring the sections twice a day for 14 days, once at sunrise and then again at sunset. Prepare a data table of the results similar to the one shown.

Day	Time	Section 1
1	sunrise	
	sunset	
2	sunrise	
	sunset	

Calculate daytime growth by subtracting the sunrise measurement from the sunset measurement of the same day. Calculate nighttime growth by subtracting the sunset measurement of one day from the sunrise measurement of the next day.

2. Pinto beans are dicots. Do the stems of other dicots grow the way pinto bean stems do? Repeat the original experiment, planting 2 pinto beans and 2 lima beans.

3. Do the stems of monocots grow like the stems of dicots? See chapter 15, "Clipped," for monocot experiments.

SHOW TIME!

Determine the location of the meristem on the stem of an outdoor shrub, such as a Japanese boxwood, waxleaf ligustrum, or euonymus. Select a stem on the shrub that has new growth at the end. Tie a string around the stem for identification. Study the diagram, then locate each **node** (a joint in a stem where a leaf is generally attached) and **internodes** (the area on the stem between two consecutive nodes).

Starting at the end of the stem, use a ruler to measure and record the length of five or more internodes on the stem. Let internode 1 be at the tip of the stem. Measure each internode every day for 7 days.

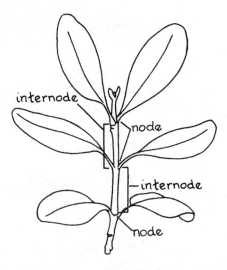

CHECK IT OUT!

An increase in the width of a stem is called *secondary growth*. Find out more about secondary growth. What is the cambium?

15

Clipped

PROBLEM

How do grass stems grow?

Materials

masking tape
marking pen
ruler

NOTE: This experiment must be performed outdoors in an area of tall grass, such as Johnson grass.

Procedure

CAUTION: Take precautions to protect yourself from insect bites.

1. Choose a stem of tall grass, but do not pick it. Attach a small piece of tape to the tip of the stem. Write the number 1 on the tape to identify the stem.

2. Locate the nodes on the stem. (The nodes are the thickened areas where

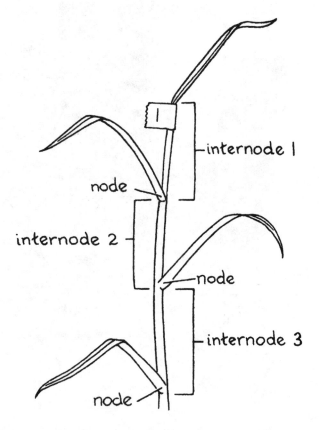

the blades of grass branch off the stem.

3. Starting at the tip of the stem, measure and record the length of three or more internodes (the area between two consecutive nodes). Call the internode at the tip of the stem internode 1.

4. Repeat step 3, using two other stems of grass. Attach a small piece of tape to the tip of each stem. Write the numbers 2 and 3 on the pieces of tape to identify these two stems.

5. Wait 2 days, then measure and record the length of each internode on all three stems.

Results

Each internode increases in length.

Why?

Upright grass stems above ground are called **culms** and are made of two parts: nodes and internodes. Nodes are solid joints where leaves are generally attached. The internodes, or areas between the nodes, are usually hollow, but may be **pithy** (soft and spongy) or solid. Generally, stems of dicot plants grow at their tips. But stems of many monocots, such as grasses, grow just above each node along the stem. When an upper section of a grass stem is cut off, the lower part of the stem continues to grow. This type of growth allows grass to survive being clipped off by lawn mowers or nibbled to the ground by various animals.

Grass Stem 1

Internode number	Final length	Minus	Starting length	Equals	Growth
1	6 inches (15 cm)	–	4 inches (10 cm)	=	2 inches (5 cm)

LET'S EXPLORE

Is there a difference in the amount of growth of different internodes on a grass stem? Use the measurements from the experiment to construct a data chart

similar to the one shown. Use the chart on page 61 to determine the difference in the amount of growth of the internodes.

SHOW TIME!

1. Is there growth both above and below a node on a grass stem? Use two pieces of masking tape about 2 inches (5 cm) long for each node in this experiment. Attach one piece of tape to the stem directly above a node, and a second piece of tape directly below the same node. Write the number 1 on both pieces of tape. Repeat the procedure, attaching two more pieces of tape above and below a second node on the same stem. Write the number 2 on these two pieces of tape. Each day for 3 or more days, measure the distance from each piece of tape to each corresponding node.

2. Does the entire internode on a grass stem grow? Choose one stem of Johnson grass or other tall grass, then use a marking pen to mark four equal sections on an internode. Mark a few more internodes in the same way. Measure and record the distance between the marks once a day for 2 days.

3. Do short grasses, such as lawn grasses, grow the same way that tall grasses do? With an adult's permission, use a spade to dig up a clump of short grass large enough to fit inside a paper cup. Choose a clump that has at least three stems, and get as many of the grass roots as possible. Plant the grass in a cup of soil. Moisten the soil with water and keep it moist throughout the experiment.

Choose one stem. Starting at the tip of the stem, use a marking pen to mark three equal sections on an internode. Mark at least two more internodes in the same way. Measure and record the distance between the marks once a day for 7 days.

CHECK IT OUT!

Grasses, such as Bermuda grass, have creeping stems that grow below and above ground. Find out more about grass stems. What are rhizomes? Stolons?

16

With and Without

PROBLEM

Is light on the soil needed for mustard seed germination?

Materials

pencil
3 egg cartons (polystyrene, not paper)
scissors
3 cups (750 ml) potting soil
mustard seeds
1-tablespoon (15-ml) measuring spoon
tap water

Procedure

1. Use the following steps to construct a closable germinating tray:
   - Use the pencil to punch a small drainage hole in the bottom of each compartment of one of the egg cartons.
   - Cut the lid off a second carton. Discard the bottom of the carton. *NOTE: Recycle discarded polystyrene.*
   - Set the first egg carton in the lid of the second carton so that the lid will catch water draining through the holes.

2. Construct an open germinating tray from the third egg carton. Repeat the previous procedure, but remove the lid from the egg carton and use that lid to collect drain water.

3. Fill the compartments of both germinating trays about half full with soil.

4. Sprinkle a few mustard seeds in each compartment of the trays.

5. Cover the seeds with about 1 tablespoon (15 ml) of soil.

6. Moisten the soil in each tray with an equal amount of water. Keep the soil in each tray moist, but not wet, during the entire experiment.

7. Close the lid of the first germinating tray. Place both trays near a window that receives light most of the day, such as a window facing south.

8. Observe the open tray daily for the first signs of plant growth.

Results

The seeds in both trays germinate.

Why?

During the last stages of seed development, the seed **dehydrates** (loses water) until it contains very little water. The embryo ceases to grow and remains inactive until the seed germinates. Thus, germination doesn't mean that a seed comes alive, but rather that it resumes the growth and development that stopped during the last stages of seed development.

Some dicot seeds, such as mustard, germinate as soon as they are in favorable conditions. Favorable conditions for mustard seeds are sufficient warmth, water, and oxygen. All the seeds in this experiment were exposed to light before being planted. Since the seeds grew in the closed tray, light on the soil was not needed for the seeds to germinate.

LET'S EXPLORE

1a. Would other dicots give the same results? Repeat the experiment, planting dicot seeds such as radish or beans. Make diagrams of both trays, indicating which type of seed is in each compartment. **Science Fair Hint:** Continue to make diagrams of the seeds in each tray

throughout the experiment to use as part of a project display.

b. Would not covering the seeds with soil affect the results? Repeat the previous experiment, filling the containers with soil. Press the seeds into the surface of the soil, but do not cover them with soil. Use a magnifying lens to observe and study the seeds daily.

c. Would monocot seeds give the same results? Repeat the previous experiments using corn kernels.

SHOW TIME!

1. Does the depth that the seeds are planted affect the results? Fill two 10-ounce (300-ml) clear plastic cups with soil. In each cup, plant 4 to 5 pinto beans at different depths so that they are visible through the side of the cup. Place one bean on the surface of the soil. Moisten the soil in each cup with water and keep the soil moist during the experiment. Set the cups near a window. Turn a large Styrofoam cup upside down and use it to cover one of the cups. Observe the seeds daily, quickly lifting and replacing the lid of the covered cup in order to limit the amount of light entering the cup. Display dated photographs and/or drawings of the seeds to represent the results.

CHECK IT OUT!

Some seeds will not germinate until they are exposed to light before planting. Plowing a field or cultivating the soil in a garden usually results in plant growth, partly because it exposes the seeds in the soil to light. Find out more about the effect of light on seed germination. What color of light is most effective in promoting germination? How does phytochrome affect germination?

17

Shady

PROBLEM

How does distance from a light source affect the amount of light received by a plant?

Materials

scissors
roll of wide paper with no designs, such as butcher paper
small houseplant about 12 inches (30 cm) tall
flashlight
yardstick (meterstick)
3 crayons of different colors
helper

Procedure

1. Cut a square of paper that is about twice as wide as the widest part of the plant.

2. Place the paper on the floor and set the plant in the center of the paper.

3. Darken the room and hold the flashlight just above the plant.

4. Ask a helper to use one of the crayons to outline the plant's shadow on the paper.

5. Move the flashlight to about 1 foot (3 m) above the plant.

6. Ask your helper to outline the shadow on the paper with a crayon of a different color.

7. Move the flashlight to about 2 feet (6 m) above the plant.

8. Again, have your helper outline the shadow on the paper with the remaining crayon.

Results

The shadow is smaller when the light is held farther above the plant.

Why?

A **shadow** is the dark area cast upon a surface by an object blocking light. The plant blocks the light coming from the flashlight. The size of the plant's shadow indicates how much light the plant blocks, and thus indicates how much light reaches the plant. A plant closer to a light casts a larger shadow. This plant receives more light than a plant that is farther away from the light and that casts a smaller shadow.

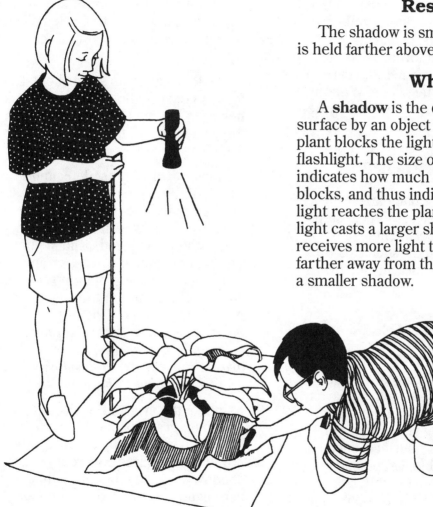

Light is very important to many plant processes, especially to photosynthesis. During photosynthesis, plants use light energy absorbed by chlorophyll in the chloroplasts to change water and carbon dioxide into food for the plants. Without enough light, plants cannot photosynthesize enough and will die.

LET'S EXPLORE

Does the shape of a plant affect the amount of light it receives? Repeat steps 1 through 4 of the experiment, using plants of different shapes, such as tall, slender cactus and an African violet with flat, spreading leaves.

SHOW TIME!

1. How does the size of a leaf affect the amount of light it receives? Ask an adult for permission to collect leaves of different sizes from indoor and outdoor plants. Place a sheet of graph paper on an outdoor surface, such as the ground or a table. Graph paper with large squares—1 inch (1.25 cm)—works best. A photocopier can be used to enlarge the squares on the paper, or use a ruler to mark a piece of typing paper into 1-inch (1.25-cm) squares.

Hold a leaf by its stem about 4 inches (10 cm) above the paper. Ask a helper to outline the shadow cast on the paper. Repeat this procedure for each leaf.

From your results, determine which of the leaves collect the most light. Prepare and display a chart showing the leaves in order from least to most light received. Take a photograph of the actual leaves, arranged in order of the amount of light received, and use the photo on the chart. *NOTE: You can perform this experiment indoors in a darkened room by holding the leaf about 4 inches (10 cm) above the paper and a flashlight about 18 inches (45 cm) above the leaf.*

2. Estimate the area of the leaf shadows drawn on graph paper in the two previous experiments by counting the number of squares covered by each shadow. Count each square that is completely covered, then estimate the

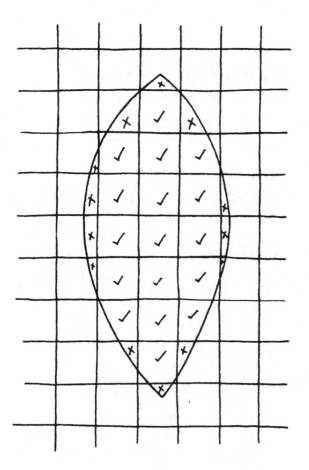

squares that are not completely covered by the following method: If half or more of a square is covered, count it as one square; if less than half the square is covered, do not count the square. For example, for the leaf shadow shown in the diagram, a check mark is placed in each square in which half or more of the square is covered. An X is placed in any square of which less than half is covered. To estimate the area, you count only the check marks. Thus, the area of the leaf shadow in the diagram equals 14 squares.

18

Light Seekers

PROBLEM

How do grass seedlings respond to light?

Materials

scissors
ruler
cardboard box about 18 × 12 × 9
    inches (45 × 30 × 22.5 cm)
9-ounce (270-ml) paper cup
potting soil
½ teaspoon (2.5 ml) grass seeds, such
    as rye, oat, or wheat
tap water
saucer
pencil
masking tape
sponge
flashlight
adult helper

Procedure

1. Ask an adult to cut a 3-inch (7.5-cm) -square opening in the center and near the top of one side of the box.

2. Fill the cup with potting soil to within 2 inches (5 cm) of the top.

3. Sprinkle the grass seeds over the surface of the soil.

4. Cover the seeds with about 1 inch (2.5 cm) of soil.

5. Moisten the soil with water.

6. Hold the cup above the saucer and use the pencil to punch two opposite holes in the bottom edge of the cup.

7. Set the cup in the saucer.

8. Put the cup and saucer inside the cardboard box on the side opposite the opening in the side of the box.

9. Close the box and seal all cracks in the box with tape to allow light to enter only through the opening.

10. Place the box near a window so that the opening in the box faces the window.

11. Allow the cup to remain undisturbed for 21 days. Keep the soil moist throughout the experiment by wetting the sponge with water and inserting it through the opening in the box. Squeeze the water from the sponge into the cup, being careful not to disturb the growing plants.

12. Make daily observations by turning the box and shining the flashlight into the opening in the box. Record a description of the growth of the grass above the surface of the soil. After observing, be sure to return the box to its original position with the opening facing the window.

NOTE: Determine the average number of hours of sunlight the box receives during the day by counting the hours between sunrise and sunset on the eleventh day of the experiment. This information will be needed for a later experiment.

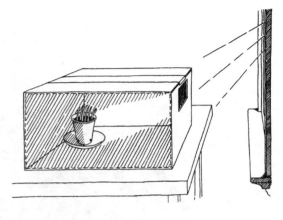

Results

The first signs of growth appear in 4 to 6 days, when straight, tubelike structures break through the soil and bend toward the opening in the box. After several more days, a single leaf breaks through the end of each tube. The tubes and leaves bend toward the opening.

Why?

Grass seeds are monocots. The tubelike structure that breaks through the soil is the coleoptile, a protective covering over the tip of a monocot's embryonic shoot. A short time after the coleoptile breaks through the surface of the soil, it stops growing, and the first leaf of the plant breaks through its tip.

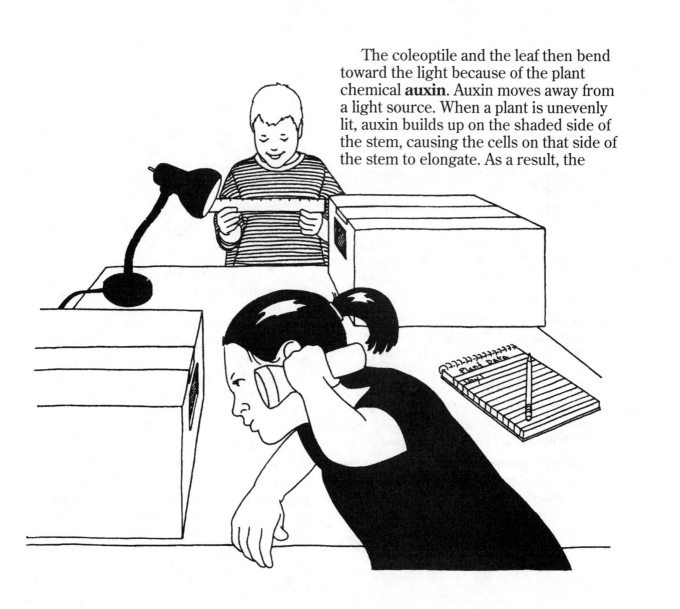

The coleoptile and the leaf then bend toward the light because of the plant chemical **auxin**. Auxin moves away from a light source. When a plant is unevenly lit, auxin builds up on the shaded side of the stem, causing the cells on that side of the stem to elongate. As a result, the plant bends toward the light. The growth response of plants to light is called **phototropism**.

LET'S EXPLORE

1. Would artificial light affect the results? Repeat the experiment, but instead of putting the box near a window, place a desk lamp about 12 inches (30 cm) in front of the opening in the box. Turn the lamp on each day for the number of hours you calculated to be the average number of hours of sunlight the box received each day in the original experiment.

2. Do other dicot seedlings behave the same way? Repeat the experiment, using pinto beans.

SHOW TIME!

Positive phototropism is growth toward light, and **negative phototropism** is growth away from light. Do roots exhibit positive or negative phototropism? Fill a 10-ounce (300-ml) clear plastic cup with potting soil. Cover half of the outside of the cup with black construction paper.

Secure the paper with transparent tape. Use a marking pen to draw a line on the cup next to the paper. Plant 6 to 8 pinto beans about ½ inch (1.25 cm) deep in the soil around the perimeter of the cup. Half the beans are to be behind the black cover. Be sure that two of the beans are planted behind but near the edges of the black paper that covers the cup. Moisten the soil with water and keep the soil moist during the experiment. At the end of 14 days, remove the black paper and compare the visible root growth in the covered and uncovered areas of the cup. Note the growth along the line marked on the cup.

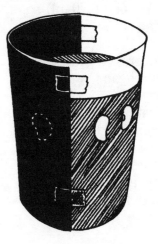

19

Tricked

PROBLEM

How does the absence of light affect bean seedlings?

Materials

masking tape
marking pen
two 9-ounce (270-ml) paper cups
potting soil
pencil
2 saucers
6 pinto beans
ruler
tap water
2 cardboard boxes at least 18 inches
   (45 cm) tall
scissors
plastic food wrap
adult helper

Procedure

1. Use the tape and marking pen to label one cup Light and the other Darkness.

2. Fill each cup three-fourths full with potting soil.

3. Use the pencil to punch two opposite holes in the bottom edge of each cup and set a cup in each saucer.

4. Plant 3 beans about ½ inch (1.25 cm) deep in the soil of each cup, placing the beans as far apart as possible.

5. Moisten the soil with water.

6. Place the cup labeled Darkness in one of the boxes. Close the box and seal all cracks in the box with tape to prevent light from entering.

7. Close the second box and seal the cracks with tape.

8. Ask an adult to make a hinged lid in the second box by cutting across

the front and two sides about 4 inches (10 cm) from the top.

9. Ask the adult to make a window in the hinged lid by cutting away the top of the lid, leaving 2 inches (5 cm) intact around the edges.

10. Cover the window in the lid with plastic wrap and secure with tape.

11. Place the cup labeled Light inside the second box.

12. Place the boxes side by side near a window.

13. Once a week for 3 weeks, open the boxes for a short time and observe the plants. Record a description of both plants, including stem length, stem shape, leaf size, and color of the stem and leaves. Keep the soil in both boxes moist.

14. At the end of 3 weeks, remove the plants from the boxes. Again, record a description of both plants.

Results

All the plants have a hook-shaped hypocotyl that breaks through the soil. The bean plants grown in darkness generally have tall, pale, spindly stems and small, pale, undeveloped leaves. The bean plants grown in light generally have greener, shorter stems that are straighter at the top, and their leaves are bigger and greener.

Why?

In nature, germination begins underground without light. The hypocotyl of a germinating bean lengthens rapidly, and a hook forms at its tip. In time, the hypocotyl breaks through the soil into the sunlight. In the presence of light, the hypocotyl straightens, raising the cotyledons and epicotyl. The plumule spreads, forming the first true leaves, which become green as chlorophyll forms. This is what happens to the beans grown in light.

However, the beans grown in darkness are tricked into behaving as though they are still underground. When each hypocotyl breaks through the soil's surface, there is no light. Lack of light causes a plant condition called **etiolation**. The hypocotyl continues to elongate rapidly, and its hook remains at the tip for a longer period of time. The leaves fail to become green and do not develop properly. Without light, the plant cannot produce chlorophyll, and its shoot is long, thin, and pale.

LET'S EXPLORE

How much light is needed to prevent etiolation? Repeat the experiment, cutting a 2-inch (5-cm) -square opening in the top of the closed box. Cover the hole with a piece of black paper. At the same time each day during the test period, lift the paper cover from the hole and allow light to enter the box for 5 minutes. Further test the quantity of light needed to prevent etiolation by using larger or smaller holes in the box and by increasing or decreasing the amount of time the light enters the box. **Science Fair Hint:** Make bar graphs of the growth of each plant to use as part of a project display.

SHOW TIME!

Does the color of the light affect growth? Obtain dark-colored cellophane in as many colors as possible. *NOTE: Use several layers of light-colored cellophane to produce a darker color.* Use clear cellophane as a control. Follow the procedure in the original experiment to plant seeds in paper cups. Prepare 1 cup for each color of cellophane used, including clear. Loosely cover each cup with cellophane, taping the edges and top of the cellophane together to form a tubelike "hat" over the cup.

Depending on the intensity of the color, the color of the cellophane will be received by the plant. Clear cellophane allows all the colors in white light to be received by the plant. Compare your results to determine how certain colors affect the bean plants' growth.

CHECK IT OUT!

The plant seems to "know" whether it is in light or in darkness. Find out more about a plant's responses to light. How do day and night length affect a plant? What is a phytochrome?

20

Up or Down?

PROBLEM

Does gravity affect plant growth of pinto beans?

Materials

paper towel
tap water
4 pinto beans
rubber band
masking tape
8-inch (20-cm) -square piece of card-
    board
permanent marking pen
1-gallon (4-liter) resealable plastic
    bag

Procedure

1. Fold the paper towel in half three times, then moisten the folded paper towel with water.

2. Place the beans on the wet towel, evenly spaced as shown.

3. Fold one end of the paper towel over the first bean. Continue folding the towel end-over-end to form a roll around the beans.

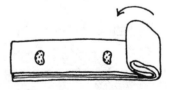

4. Wrap the rubber band around the bean roll.

5. Tape the bean roll to the center of the cardboard.

6. Draw an arrow on the cardboard above one of the open ends of the bean roll.

7. Place the cardboard inside the plastic bag so that the arrow points toward the open end of the bag. Seal the bag.

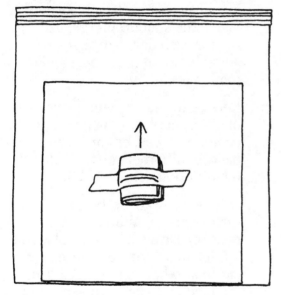

8. Tape the bag in an upright position to any stationary vertical object that allows a good view of the bag, such as a window.

9. Observe the bean roll as often as possible during each day for 7 days or until roots and stems extend from the end(s) of the bean roll.

Results

The stems of the plants in the bean roll grow upward and the roots grow downward.

Why?

As you learned in chapter 18, "Light Seekers," plants grow in certain directions because of the plant chemical auxin. Auxin makes plant cells elongate. The longer cells on one side then cause the plant to bend toward the shorter side. Different types of cells respond differently to the presence of this chemical. An increase in auxin increases the growth of stem cells, but prevents the growth of root cells.

Gravity pulls auxin down toward the lowest part of the stems and roots of a plant. More growth occurs in the cells on the lower side of the stem, and less growth in the cells on the lower side of the root. The result is that the stem bends up and the roots bend down. The growth response of plants to gravity is called **geotropism**. Since stems grow in a direction opposite to the pull of gravity, they have a **negative geotropism,** while roots have a **positive geotropism.**

LET'S EXPLORE

Do stems and roots continue to be affected by gravity as they grow? Repeat the experiment, preparing 4 bean roll bags. Use a protractor to draw a 6-inch (15-cm) -diameter circle on the cardboard in each bag. Make a mark every 10° around each circle. When the stems are about 2 inches (5 cm) long, change the position of three of the bags so that the arrows on the bags point down, right, and left. Let the fourth bag, the control bag, remain with its arrow pointing up. Make daily observations for 7 days, using the circles to compare the change in the direction of each plant's stems and roots. **Science Fair Hint:** Take photographs to represent the procedure and results of the experiment.

SHOW TIME!

1a. Most plants grow on the side of a hill in the same up-and-down direction as plants on a flat surface.

Demonstrate this by filling a shallow pan with about 2 inches (5 cm) of potting soil. Plant 6 to 8 pinto beans in the soil, and moisten the soil with water. Stand a toothpick in the soil vertically next to each bean. Prop up one end of the pan by placing a ball of clay at each corner. When the shoots emerge, use a protractor each day to measure the angle between the shoots and the toothpicks.

b. Repeat the experiment, using seeds of different plants, such as squash, cucumber, lima, or corn. Use toothpicks of different colors to identify the different seeds used.

2. Does gravity affect the growth of mature plants? With an adult's permission, lay a small houseplant on its side in a dark closet or under a cardboard box to prevent it from responding to light. Observe the position of the stems and leaves after 1 week and again 1 week later. Add water as needed to keep the soil moist. At the end of 3 weeks, carefully remove the soil from around the roots and observe their direction in relationship to the direction of the stems. Take a photograph of the plant at the beginning of the experiment and each time you observe the plant.

Glossary

absorb To take in.

aerial Above ground.

angiosperms Flowering plants that have a vascular system, have covered seeds, and are divided into two groups, monocots and dicots.

auxin A plant chemical that causes plant cells to elongate.

beans Angiosperm seeds.

carbon dioxide A gas in the air that is changed into food for the plant through photosynthesis.

carotenes Yellow or orange pigments located in the chloroplasts of plants.

cell The part of an organism that is the smallest part that can exist on its own.

cell membrane The thin, filmlike outer layer of a cell that holds the cell together, separates it from its environment, and allows materials to pass into and out of it.

cell wall The stiff outer layer of a plant cell.

chemical change A change that produces one or more substances that are different from those present before the change.

chlorophyll A green pigment found in plant chloroplasts that enables plants to use light energy to make food through photosynthesis.

chloroplast A green body found in plant cells that contains chlorophyll and in which food for the plant is made.

chlorosis The loss of green color in plants.

coleoptile The protective covering over the plumule in a monocot embryo.

coleorhiza The protective covering over the radicle in a monocot embryo.

complete flower A flower containing petals, sepals, stamens, and a pistil.

concentrated To be crowded with a material.

conifers Nonflowering plants, usually trees with small, evergreen, needle-shaped leaves, that reproduce by forming cones.

cotyledon A simple leaf that stores food for a developing plant; also called a seed leaf.

culms Upright grass stems above ground.

cuticle The waxy covering of most plants that prevents excessive loss of water by slowing down the passage of water vapor through the epidermis.

cytoplasm The jellylike material, made mostly of water, that fills a cell.

dehydrate To lose water.

dicotyledon or **dicot** An angiosperm having two cotyledons and (usually) flower parts occurring in multiples of four or five.

diffusion The spreading out of a material from a concentrated area to a less concentrated area.

egg Female reproductive cell.

elongate To grow longer.

embryo An organism in its earliest stages of development, such as an undeveloped plant inside a seed.

embryonic Undeveloped.

endosperm The nourishing tissue for the developing embryo inside angiosperm seeds.

epicotyl The part of a plant embryo, located above the hypocotyl, that develops into the plant's stem, leaves, flowers, and fruit.

etiolation A condition in plants characterized by rapid lengthening of the stem, small undeveloped leaves, a bent hypocotyl hook that remains at the tip of the shoot longer than usual, and lack of chlorophyll, all due to lack of light.

evaporate   To change from a liquid to a gas.

evergreen   Having leaves that remain green all through the year.

emerge   To come out.

fertilization   The joining of an egg and a sperm.

flower   The part of a flowering plant that contains the reproductive organs.

fruit   The enlarged ovary of a flowering plant in which the seeds are contained.

geotropism   The growth response of plants to gravity.

germination   The process by which a seed sprouts.

germination starting time (GST)   As defined in this book, the time it takes from planting a seed to the first signs of hypocotyl growth.

germination time (GT)   As defined in this book, the time it takes from planting a seed to the end of germination, determined by the time it takes for the epicotyl to fully emerge from the cotyledons.

gravity   The force that pulls things toward the center of the earth.

hilum   The scar on a seed coat where the ovary was attached to the ovule.

humidity   Wetness of the air.

hydrophilic   Having an attraction for water.

hypocotyl   The part of a plant embryo that develops into the lower stem and root.

imbibe   To absorb.

imbibition   The process by which a hydrophilic, porous material absorbs water.

incomplete flower   A flower that is missing one or more of these flower parts: petals, sepals, stamens, and/or pistil.

internode   The area on a plant stem between two consecutive nodes.

leaf   The main food-producing organ of a plant.

matter   The substance of which any object is made.

meristem   Plant tissue made up of meristematic cells.

meristematic cells   Cells that divide and produce other, similar cells.

micropyle   The small opening in the wall of an ovule through which a pollen tube enters.

mitochondria (singular **mitochondrion**)   The power stations of a cell, where food and oxygen react to produce the energy needed for the cell to work and live.

mitosis   The process by which cell parts duplicate themselves and then divide into two separate cells.

molecule   The smallest particle of a substance that retains the properties of the substance.

monocotyledon or **monocot**   An angiosperm having one cotyledon and (usually) flower parts occurring in multiples of three.

nectar   A sugary liquid substance produced by many flowers at the base of their petals that aids in attracting insects and other pollinators.

negative geotropism   Plant growth in the opposite direction of the pull of gravity.

negative phototropism   The growth of a plant away from light.

node   A joint in a plant stem where a leaf is generally attached.

nonvascular plants   Plants that do not have a vascular system.

nucleus   The control center of a cell that directs all the cell's activities.

nutrients   Materials needed for the life and growth of living organisms.

organ   A structure consisting of tissues grouped together to perform a specific function or functions.

organisms   All living things, including people, plants, animals, and tiny living things called bacteria and fungi.

ovary   The rounded base of a pistil which contains ovules.

ovules   Seedlike parts within a flower's ovary that contain eggs and ripen into seeds when fertilized.

oxygen   A gas in the air.

perimeter   The measurement of a boundary.

petals   Leaflike structures, often brightly colored, that surround and help protect a flower's reproductive organs, aid in attracting insects and other pollinators, and contain organs that produce nectar.

phloem tubes   Vascular tubes that transport sap containing water and food manufactured in the leaves of a plant upward and downward to other parts of the plant.

photosynthesis   The process by which plants use light energy trapped by chlorophyll to change water and carbon dioxide into food for the plant.

phototropism   The growth response of plants to light. See also **negative phototropism** and **positive phototropism.**

pigments   Materials that absorb, reflect, and transmit visible light.

pistil   The female reproductive organ of a flowering plant.

pithy   Soft and spongy.

plumule   The embryonic shoot tip that consists of several tiny, immature leaves that at maturity form the first true leaves.

pollen cone   A small cone that contains pollen and forms in groups at the tips of the branches of conifers.

pollen grains   The yellow dustlike powder produced by stamens that contain sperm.

pollen tube   A tube formed by pollen grains when they grow down the style of a pistil.

pollination   The process by which pollen grains are transferred from a flower's stamens to its pistil.

porous   Capable of being passed through by water, air, or light.

positive geotropism   Plant growth in the direction of the pull of gravity.

positive phototropism   The growth of a plant toward light.

propagate   To produce new organisms.

radicle   The part of a plant embryo, located at the tip of the hypocotyl, that develops into the plant's root system.

receptacle   The top of the flower stem supporting the reproductive organs.

reflect   To bounce back.

reproductive organs   The organs of a plant that produce more plants.

roots   Special organs that anchor a plant, absorb water and minerals, and, sometimes, store food.

root system   The subterranean part of a plant that is made of many branching roots.

sap A liquid containing water and minerals or food that moves through a plant's vascular system.

seed A ripened ovule that contains the embryo and a stored food supply, and that is protected by a seed coat.

seed coat The outer protective covering of a seed that is formed by the wall of an ovule.

seed cone A cone that contains seeds and usually forms as a single cone away from the tips of branches of conifers.

seed dispersal The process by which seeds are scattered.

seedling A young plant grown from a seed.

sepals Leaflike structures, usually green, that surround and protect a flower before it opens.

shadow The dark area cast upon a surface by an object blocking light.

shoot The part of a plant that grows above ground.

shoot system The aerial part of a plant consisting of the shoot.

specialized cell A cell that performs a special function, such as growth or absorbing water.

spectrophotometer An instrument used to determine the colors of light that materials, such as pigment, absorb and transmit.

sperm Male reproductive cell.

sprout To begin to grow.

stamen The male reproductive organ of a flowering plant.

stem A plant organ that supports the leaves and flowers of a plant and transports water, minerals, and food throughout the plant.

stigma The sticky top part of a pistil that holds pollen grains that land on it.

style The tubelike structure of a pistil that supports the stigma and connects it with the ovary.

subterranean Below ground.

tissue A group of specialized cells that perform a similar task.

transmit To pass through.

transpiration The process by which plants lose water through their leaves.

transport To carry from one place to another.

turgidity The firmness of a plant cell due to turgor pressure.

turgor pressure The internal pressure inside a plant cell due to the presence of water.

vascular plants Plants that have a vascular system.

vascular system A system containing bundles of vascular tubes that transport sap.

vascular tubes Tubes in a plant's vascular system that transport sap throughout the plant; xylem tubes and phloem tubes.

veins In a leaf, the conducting structures made of bundles of vascular tubes forming the framework through which sap flows.

visible light Colors of light that can be seen by the human eye.

volume The amount of space taken up by an object.

water vapor Water in the gas state.

wilt To become limp; decrease in turgidity.

xanthophylls Pale yellow pigments located in the chloroplasts of plants.

xylem tubes Vascular tubes that transport sap containing water and minerals upward from the roots through the plant.

zygote A fertilized egg.

Index

stigma, 28, 29, 30, 87
style, 28, 29, 30, 87
plumule, 54
  definition of, 38, 86
  diagram of, 38
  growth of, 49, 53, 78
pollen grains, 33
  definition of, 26, 86
  model of, 25–26
pollen tube:
  definition of, 29, 86
  model of, 28–30
pollination:
  definition of, 26, 86
propagation:
  definition of, 45, 86
radicle:
  definition of, 37, 86
  diagram, 37
  growth of, 49, 53
root, 54
  definition of, 7, 86
root system:
  definition of, 49, 86
  effect of gravity on, 82–83
  receptacle, 31, 86
  roots, 7, 54, 80–83, 86
sap:
  definition of, 10, 13, 14
  movement of, 13, 14
seeds:
  conifer, 32–35
  cotyledons, 37
  coleoptile, 49, 53, 84
  coleorhiza, 49, 53, 84
  corn, 52–55
  definition of, 37, 85
  dicotyledon (*see* dicotyledon)
  dispersal of, 31

dormant, 46
epicotyl 38, 84
formation of, 28–31
germination of, 44–51, 64–67
hilum, 37, 85
hypocotyl, 37, 85
imbibition of, 40–43
monocotyledon, 27, 52–55, 85
seed coat, 36, 37, 38–39, 43,
  45, 53
structure, 36–39
seedlings:
  dicotyledon (*see* dicotyledon)
  definition of, 49, 87
  growth of, 48–51, 72–83
sepals:
  definition of, 26, 87
  models of, 24–27, 31
shoot system:
  definition of, 49, 87
  shoot (*see* shoot)
shoot:
  definition of, 37, 87
  development of, 49
  growth of, 73, 79, 82
  shoot system, 49, 87
spectrophotometer:
  definition of, 19, 87
  model of, 19
sperm:
  definition of, 26, 87
  formation of, 33
stamen:
  definition of, 26, 87
  model of, 25–26, 31
stems:
  definition of, 7, 87
  formation of, 38
  growth of, 54, 56–63, 72–83

internodes, 56–64, 85
model of, 26, 31
nodes, 58, 60, 61, 85
secondary growth, 58
stigma:
  definition of, 29, 87
  model of, 28–30
tissue:
  definition of, 7, 87
  meristem, 57, 85
  model of, 7
transpiration:
  definition of, 14, 87
  experiments, 12–15
turgor pressure:
  definition of, 15, 87
  experiment, 15
vascular plants:
  angiosperm (*see* angiosperm)
  definition of, 10, 87
  leaf of, 12
vascular system:
  definition of, 10, 87
  vascular tubes, 10, 12–15,
    86, 87
vascular tubes:
  definition of, 10, 87
  phloem tubes, 13, 86
  leaf, 12–13
  xylem tubes, 12–15, 87
xylem tubes:
  definition of, 12, 13, 87
  experiments, 12–15
  structure of, 13
zygote:
  definition of, 29, 87
  formation of, 29